MAX.INCOME.PLAYBOOK®

21 Winning Plays For Retirement Streams Of Money

Bruce Weinstein

ISBN: 9798990860629
Library of Congress Control Number:
Designed by
INDIE BOOKS INTERNATIONAL®, INC.
2511 WOODLANDS WAY
OCEANSIDE, CA 92054
www.indiebooksintl.com

Acknowledgements

I would first like to acknowledge the life insurance agents across the United States. Every day, someone is telling our clients life insurance is a horrible investment and why they don't need it. Many times, these individuals are not even licensed and have never handed a check for millions of dollars the loved ones of someone who has passed away. For all of you who believe in the product and know how to use it, please continue to implement and fight for what is in the client's best interest. The financial world needs you.

To my mentors, Jason and Art Sanger, Bob Castiglione, Nelson Nash, Todd Langford, and Kim Butler: I can't express how much I'm humbled by your brilliance. Thank you so much for the time you have put into teaching us how money works and the truth about it. There is so much misinformation in the media that sometimes going back to my notes from symposiums and seminars keeps me focused on my never-ending journey to educate pre-retirees and retirees on how to plan for retirement income streams.

To Barney Sidler, who acted as a mentor as well as a father to me when I started: Your guidance and support gave me the foundation I needed to succeed in this industry. I am forever grateful for your wisdom and kindness.

To my friend and colleague Phil Bodine: Traveling back and forth from California to Arizona and around the United States to learn, our talks and mutual motivation are just as important as formal education. I love you, my brother.

To my beautiful daughter and successor of my business, Skylar: You amaze me every day. I'm so proud of you and who you've become. I don't think I could have lasted this long without you. To my other children, Michael, a soon to be MD, and Jack, my beautiful son whose strength as a proud gay man gives me more courage than you can imagine: You remind me so much of myself at 23 years old when I started.

Last but most importantly my amazing wife Jenny, who without, I wouldn't still be in this business. As a young man starting out with little education in this industry, she never let me quit. She is my beautiful angel.

This is my first book but not my last. I hope you enjoy it.

CONTENTS

CONTENTS

PREFACE

We have to plan for the "what-ifs" in life. In 2004, I sold an insurance policy to my best friend, and you never really want to plan for the event happening.

You just plan for the what-ifs. In 2010, after a long battle with cancer, I had to deliver one of the largest death claims ever to his family. I have never felt that way before because I knew that the check was my last connection to my best friend.

Not only are these clients, they are some of our closest friends. We can do all this business with people and make a nice career for ourselves, but that is a side benefit when you look at the real impact of what we do for people.

That moment in my career made me a different person. I was able to identify the real reason why I am in this business. When I sat down with my best friend in 2004, I had an obligation to him, not only as a friend, but professionally, to protect him and his family. It is by far what has kept me around for twenty-five years in this business.

We have an obligation as financial advisors to take care of everybody in the exact same way in this business. Or, at least, give them the opportunity to understand this process involves much more than money saved in an account. It's about your life.

At Premier Southwest Benefits Group, we specialize in helping people integrate and coordinate all their financial and insurance decisions. My vision was to bring all the insurance companies and the investment institutions under one umbrella so our clients can establish a comprehensive program that incorporates and integrates all their insurances with their investments.

The world of retirement planning has changed dramatically. In the past, you could work hard and let time and hard work be your friend. Today, you have outside influences, where a plan that you thought would work unravels because of the current economic scenario.

There are two different phases in one's life. One is the accumulation phase, and one is the distribution phase. When you are accumulating wealth, you are looking at how much money you will have. When you get to the distribution phase, you are looking at income. How much income am I going to have in order to accomplish my goals, my needs, and my desires through retirement? That is a different process.

We are trying to get to know the client deeply. There are dollars that they have. However, it is more important to find out what they are trying to do in life. Planning is more than the money they have saved.

We want to provide clients with the confidence that they are not going to outlive their money. That confidence comes from knowing the client.

We owe it to our clients to continue our education and give them the best of what we have.

Things are always changing, and we need to be on the cutting edge so we can know what is going on and how to adapt to it.

When you attend continuing education to keep abreast of what is going on, you learn new strategies that you could teach your clients. We feel obligated to be able to know what those new options are.

The more I can learn, the more I can teach my clients, which makes both of us better in the long run.

We need to continually be on top of our game. Some of the strategies that are in place today were not around ten years ago. It puts my client in the best situation.

Our business model is contingent upon what a client's need is, not what another entity says.

I have always felt that if we put our client's interest first with regards to their dreams, their goals, their wishes throughout their retirement, it gives us the best opportunity for the best outcome.

These people are our clients, and more importantly, they are our friends.

Bruce Weinstein, 2024

1 |

WHY IF YOU DON'T PLAY YOU WILL NEVER WIN

The old joke goes that a penny saved is a lousy retirement plan. Yet many people and most advisors that are out there today talk to people about accumulation of wealth. They promise to save the person a pile of money which will help that person climb that mountain to retirement.

Of course, those advisors will accomplish that at a certain rate of return. The way they go about accomplishing this is through this mathematical equation: if you have X amount of dollars, then you need to save Y amount to hit that retirement goal. Well, when you follow that equation, you are giving up a part of your lifestyle to save that money. You should want to understand how that lifestyle would play out for you.

Once you get to the top of the mountain with all the money that you have saved, you will be retiring those assets. The conversation becomes more than that delta of savings.

If you can get the same income coming down the mountain as the income you worked for going up the mountain, you have more of an idea what both your current and future lifestyles are going to be. You then have information to compare income to your lifestyle. What can those assets provide for a lifestyle? And what if I can make choices now to leverage those assets as I come down the mountain?

It makes sense to understand how income streams work to direct whatever money you are saving today for the lifestyle you wish to have tomorrow. Instead of learning about accumulation, you should be considering where to direct those savings today to create maximum income later from those assets.

When you retire the assets, aka start to draw down from them, those assets support your future lifestyle. Think of this another way: it is not about how much money you have; it is about what kind of income you can get out of that money and what strategies are in place to maximize that income.

Here is a simple example to illustrate this point. Most people think a 401(k) plan is the eighth wonder of the world. This is because of terms like compound interest and tax-deferred savings. Maybe your accountant has told you to always put the maximum into a 401(k). This is a situation familiar to everyone.

I like to start my conversation with clients in this way, "How many millionaires do you know out there?" (And we will get to that in another story.)

"Zero."

"And you currently have all your money in your 401(k)?"

"Yes."

"So, can I pick on your 401(k) for a minute?"

"Sure. Please do, because that's why I'm here to see you."

"Let's just say you continue on this path, and you accumulate every year and reach a million dollars in assets. Let's talk about what a sustainable withdrawal rate is on a million dollars. Has your advisor talked to you about that?"

"They haven't"

Financial advisors use systems to simulate how much of a sustainable withdrawal you can pull out of our income, and that number is typically only 3 to 4 percent for a married couple, because you have to sustain an income for two lives versus one.

Let's say for your income as a married couple, you could sustain a strong 4 percent withdrawal for the rest of both of your lives. With what the probabilities of investment success are, that income stream is at best about $40,000 a year. And at that point in time, it becomes the tax payment conversation.

Unfortunately, you will pay taxes on that money no matter what. Your 401(k) is actually a tax-deferral plan, and income taxes due on that 401(k) money in retirement can reduce your yearly net amount to $28,000. In this example, a million dollars is only providing $28,000 a year of income. How do you feel about $28,000 a year of income for the rest of your life?

Most of my clients, and probably you reading this, do not feel good at all about that. What if, instead, it was $100,000 a year off a million dollars of savings or $75,000 a year off of $750,000, and you invest the balance ($250,000) somewhere else? You have the same million dollars of savings, but now you have split it into two different places. What if there was an example or two that would create double to triple the income with less risk?

Maximum income is all about how much income you have, not how much accumulation you have. And hopefully you can see the difference.

The question becomes how do you get there?

2 |

MY PHOENIX RISING COMEBACK STORY

Before I give you a guided tour of how to maximize income, you should meet the tour guide. I like to say mine is a "phoenix rising from the ashes" comeback story.

In 1983, I decided to attend Arizona State University, relocating from a suburb in Chicago. I ended up staying.

As I went through the process of trying to get a job at the Arizona State job fairs, not one person was interested in me. I remember having a great conversation with Baxter Tranel. I knew they were in a suburb right by where I lived back in Chicago. I talked to them for forty-five minutes, only to never hear from them again.

I answered a blind ad in the paper, which got me into this business. Even to this day, I have no idea how that happened, but it happened. I got in the business in 1988. And for the first few years, I was just trying to find my way in the business.

In 1989, my father gave me a call, asking me if I wanted to go into business with him. It was going to be either me or my brother. I asked my father, "Well, how much time do I have to give you to answer that?"

"You have two weeks," my dad said.

"I'll answer you right now," I replied.

The answer was no, which led me to stay in Arizona and continue along my path. And in 1990, my college sweetheart, who is now my wife of thirty years, moved to Chicago.

I went back to Chicago. I wanted to stay with the same company, but unfortunately, they didn't have an office there.

Luckily, my dad introduced me to one of his clients who was a partner with my uncle, who had his own financial services company. My dad said, "This guy will take you underneath his wing."

His name is Barney Siller. He is one of my mentors, a survivor of the Holocaust, and one of the greatest guys I ever met, like a second father to me. His niche was in the medical market, which included physicians and surgeons. This was my first real parlay into the business.

In 1997, my wife and I moved back to Arizona. I wanted to be in a location where I could see my friends from college, including some of my fraternity brothers and some of my best friends. This move also led me to the same broker dealer in the same insurance company that I worked with in Chicago.

However, that stint was short lived, but led me to Guardian Life Insurance Company. This organization had a huge impact on my life because they introduced me to the LEAP System and my next mentor. His name is Art Sanger, and he taught me one of the most important ideas that impacted my career: math is not money and money is not math.

The LEAP System looks at protection, growth and savings of an individual's financial life. It helps not only to see every aspect of a financial picture, but also to help identify lost opportunities of financial growth. This can be something as simple as bank fees that add up over time and could have been used somewhere else to help mitigate market volatility or otherwise minimize wealth erosion.

Instead of looking at individual silos of expenses and income, it looks at finances as a part of your entire financial existence. Because your life is made up of more than a balance sheet.

Art had us take out a piece of paper and write down a few numbers. He said, "Here's an average rate of return: 25 percent. Use that percentage for calculations of savings growth over a four-year period."

In this example, he asked us to start with $100,000. When we did the math, we ended up with the same amount. The average rate of return was 25 percent, but the actual rate of return was zero. That taught me something that was an aha moment in my career.

Art is still a friend of mine. I went into business with his son, Jason Sanger, with a company called Wealth Building Cornerstones, which I use every single day to create maximum income streams for my clients. Jason has become a mentor of mine. Art said, "Jason's the smartest kid I know."

While I still believe no one is as smart as Art Sanger, Jason is in the same league. I love both of them dearly and owe part of my career success to them.

In 2003, I decided that instead of working for someone else, I wanted to be an independent advisor. Because of this decision, I formed Premier Southwest Benefits Group.

When I branched off on my own, I focused my efforts strictly on the LEAP System, and creating maximum income streams for people in retirement. This is still my focus today.

One of the greatest things to happen to me in my career, besides this focus, was when my daughter, Skylar, who was a sophomore in college, called me up, said, "Dad, I don't want to be a teacher. I want to go into your business."

"Are you serious?"

"Yes. Should I go into finance?"

"Skylar, everything they teach you in college is never going to work in finance because it's not always applicable in the real world. Instead, I would go into marketing because marketing is going to teach you how to be an entrepreneur and a business owner, plus you are going to get the skillset of sales."

That conversation put Skylar on a new path, and has helped me out the most in my business. Her insight as a marketer is why I am successful - because she understands that people do not line up at my door to buy investments from me or buy insurance from me. I have to go find them, and I have to court them into understanding why we are different than everybody else.

But that one question that she asked, should I go into finance, changed both of our trajectories.

3 |

THE ONLY MONEY YOU SHOULD HAVE ON THE SIDELINES

In the words of author Robert Kiyosaki, "It's easier to stand on the sidelines, criticize, and say why you shouldn't do something. The sidelines are crowded. Get in the game."

In life, most people believe that the way to win is to get in the game and not stay on the sidelines. In the finance world, that belief is slightly different. There is power in having money on the sidelines.

Just like in sports, having players on the sidelines gives you insurance if something goes awry in the game itself. And something can always go awry in the game of life.

But what money goes to the sidelines and what money should be in the game?

I want to be clear as you read this book. Everything that I am telling you is something that came from my mentors. As a professional financial advisor that specializes in income streams, these strategies are not ones that I invented. I learned them, and that is the purpose of this book: to teach you strategies that will work because they have been tested over and over again.

Once you get to retirement, there are three things to worry about in this exact order: income, liquidity and legacy. Money that is put on the sidelines has to be there both before and after retirement.

The rule of thumb is to always strive to have from six months to one year's worth of income ready to come into the game if needed. If you make a large amount of income, say $300,000 to $400,000 a year, at least $100,000 a year should be on the sidelines. Yes, you read that correctly. A good amount of money has to be set off on the sidelines for unexpected things that could happen. This includes things like technological change that are wealth eroding factors. This goes back to the LEAP System.

You will need to buy a new computer as it ages. You will need to buy a new phone every three or four years, whether you like it or not, because phones are built to be replaced. Technological change is consistently happening and when you retire, will have a propensity to consume your wealth.

There are other factors that will consume your wealth. You may need to replace your roof or water heater in your home that you have paid off. If you break your asset plan and the flow of money in versus out, the plan no longer serves you. The money placed on the sidelines can then be used to either keep the plan in place or replace the money depleted from the plan.

Most people have a small amount of savings because the belief is money always needs to be invested. At the time of book publication, the U.S. economy is allowing a high interest rate period of time where savings can be accumulating some interest. However, in the past, the interest earned on savings was near zero, so it may have felt like savings would not be the best choice.

As an example, in a period of high interest rates, if you have $100,000 on the sidelines and you are making $5,000 of interest on that amount, that equates to $5,000 a year of money that can be put somewhere else to create more wealth for your future.

In periods of high interest, you can and should take advantage of that. But whether it is a high interest rate period or not, it is still imperative to always have a certain amount of money on the sidelines, accessible in liquid accounts, in case there are wealth-eroding factors or events which go beyond taxes.

Owing the IRS is never a good position to be in, and neither is being unprepared for unexpected expenses. You never want to break into retirement accounts or derail income plans because there was not enough cash to pay for unexpected or unforeseen issues.

There are other things that need protecting within your retirement assets as well, which we will explore next.

4 |
PROTECT THE ESTATE
PROTECT THE NET

Sports are used in many business analogies and are applicable to retirement conversations as well.

In this book "the Max.Income.Playbook®", I use the analogy of a hockey goalie protecting the net. The goalie's job is to stop pucks from going into the net.

What I mean by your net in the retirement analogy would be your assets, everything that is a part of your estate. If you go back to the 15th, 16th, or even 17th century—in the time of royalty and extremely wealthy landowners—their wealth would be tied to their land and castle.

In the LEAP System, my mentor Robert "Bob" Castiglione always talked about the concept of protecting the castle. In the times of castles, there was a moat to protect it. What moat do you have around your castle? Your castle (i.e. your wealth) could be your house and your 401(k). It could be in other assets, such as a business or investment property, but you have an estate. And that estate needs to be protected.

There are two key ways to protect your estate, both equally important. The first way to protect your estate is to keep it from going to probate when you pass away. When you go into probate, it opens the possibility of others making decisions about your estate on your behalf.

If you are in an accident, who will make decisions for you? When you pass away, who will determine how your assets are distributed? Either you have made these decisions, or the state will decide for you.

Probate becomes problematic because it involves the court system, which could include an attorney and a fiduciary, both of which cost money that the estate pays for. It also means that distribution of your estate is delayed while the estate is in probate to make sure any debts against the estate are paid and to determine asset distribution. Thus, not handling advance preparation by putting an effective estate plan in place results in unnecessary costs and delays.

The other key way to protect your estate is with life insurance. Much of the assets that you own are not necessarily liquid. Life insurance will be discussed in more detail later in the book since it is part of the moat around your castle. This is because of certain rules that affect life insurance. This includes having an asset which can never be owned without a beneficiary.

You may argue that real estate has an assumed beneficiary if you, for example, own a house with your spouse. But what happens if you both die simultaneously? Who does the house go to? There needs to be additional protection in place to fortify your moat.

Creating a trust is another good way to protect your castle. However, you need to work with an estate planning attorney or trust preparer to put a proper trust in order.

Something is not better than nothing when it comes having your estate in order. Whether you go to an attorney, a trust preparer, LegalZoom, or take something off of the internet, the most important thing is to take that first step to protect your castle. If you do not protect your castle, you are allowing a potential invasion of government agencies, other wealthy institutions or large corporations. And they will easily breach your castle.

If you watch sports like NFL or the NHL, defense is what always wins Super Bowls and Stanley Cups. In hockey, a great goaltender is the difference between a team winning the Stanley Cup or not. If you think about what winning in your financial life would look like, it is how you set up retirement income streams to support the retirement lifestyle you end up living, as well as how well you defend your wealth with an estate plan, insurance and other strategies.

How are you keeping pucks from getting in the net when something unplanned happens? For instance, do you have insurance in place if you need long-term care? There is a rule referred to by many as the 70/70 rule: by age seventy, 70 percent of people in the US will have some sort of long-term care or health situation. If it happens to you, will you be protected or will you have put your assets at risk because your goaltender was not in place?

In sports, the best defense is a strong and seasoned goaltender guarding the net—which creates the best offense. In life, your offense allows you to participate in the accumulation of your wealth, to organize that wealth, and provide the freedom to acquire assets that will make sense for your future. Part of the protection of your net is having an estate plan as well as having insurance, including long-term care insurance.

But it doesn't end there.

5 |

PROTECT THE QB AND OFFENSIVE COORDINATOR

Do you recall the famous opening monologue in the movie The Blind Side? This occurs when the character Leigh Anne Tuohy, played by Academy Award winner Sandra Bullock, talks about who is protected first and second in the game of football.

Tuohy says, "As any housewife knows, the first check you write is for the mortgage, but the second is for the insurance."

In football, the left tackle is the insurance that protects the quarterback from what he cannot see, or his blind side.

There is another vital role that is not on the field of play, but still affects the outcome of the game: the offensive coordinator. You may not always think about the offensive coordinator because that person is on the sidelines. But this role is vital in ensuring the plays are created and executed fully. In the Max.Income.Playbook®, your offensive coordinator is your financial advisor. This role is paramount in moving the ball forward (your wealth) and getting across the finish line (whether to accumulate wealth, maximize income or plan for your future).

Who is coordinating your financial offensive plays? Today, there are many two-income families. In the game of life, you have one member who is the quarterback and one who is the offensive coordinator, and this switches between partners throughout the marriage. That also means either person can be vulnerable. Because of rising costs and economic situations that come up, many couples find it impossible not to have two incomes.

One of the things that my mentor, Barney Siller, taught me when I was starting out in this business and we worked with doctors, was to use the image of an ATM. Imagine you have an ATM in your basement spitting out $20 bills every minute. How much insurance would you buy to protect that ATM?

The answer would be as much as you can get. Are you that much different than an ATM? You are creating money with your work you go to every day. You use that money to pay for expenses, to live in your house, to eat food, to live a certain lifestyle.

You do not have to buy insurance. But you are one of the most important assets in your wealth accumulation. Maybe you will earn enough money to provide for your family when you die. But you probably do not have enough disability insurance if you get sick and need to be cared for.

Most people do not think about the situation of getting older, especially when in their prime. From the statistic mentioned in the previous chapter, there is a 70 percent chance of needing additional care after the age of seventy. You may think that if something happens, you would be able to stay in your home. Unfortunately, the U.S. $92 billion assisted living facility industry has a different opinion, according to the U.S. Assisted Living Facility Market Size & Share Report" from Grand View Research.

According to the Alzheimer's Association, nearly seven million people in the U.S. are living with Alzheimer's. And of the total cost of caring for someone with the disease, 70 percent is absorbed by the family.

This is just one possible disease that can affect your wealth stability and a good reason to consider an insurance option. This helps to protect the money-makers (the ATMs) that are building the wealth for the family. If you look at what you need to protect, you can learn how to protect it.

When I played football, I had two main responsibilities: to get the ball to the quarterback and to call audibles when the situation changed on the offensive line, which is inevitable. Other players had other jobs that I trusted, such as opening a hole for the running backs or blocking for a forward pass. It allowed me to focus on my job all of the time which was always getting the ball to the quarterback. Because without me giving the ball to the quarterback, there could be no play.

If something happens to you, what do you have in play to protect your wealth? Not sure if this might happen to you? Let me share a story with you.

6 |

HOW INSURANCE SAVED MY ASSETS

Murphy's Law states that anything that can go wrong will go wrong And some people say Murphy was an optimist.

While life may feel that way, by and large, planning and due diligence can prevent most accidents (otherwise planes would drop out of the sky, the kitchen would always catch fire, etc.). But Murphy is sitting on the sidelines, waiting for the opportunity to strike.

When I went independent in 2005, I started accumulating wealth in real estate. I had a partner that was a general contractor. Within six months, we were up a half a million dollars. Real estate was easy, because homeowners used signature loans, comprised of checking credit, signing a statement, and quickly getting a home equity credit line, or a refinance option to access equity from the property.

Houses were being built at a rapid pace at the time. So much so that banks could not keep up with processing the applications. Like everyone else, I also took advantage of that. I used my home equity to expand and buy real estate. I did not have that much money, but I did put money into different assets. With this phenomenon, I decided to go full force into real estate.

In 2008, I had been building wealth through real estate and felt pretty secure. Then the financial markets started to crash because of the signature loans. Because of this, I got stuck between a proverbial house brick and a hard place. The bank froze my home equity credit line. I had no access to capital whatsoever, with $430,000 out on it already. My house dropped in value by 50 percent. The only thing I had left was my life insurance policy, which had $157,000 in cash value. Everything else was gone because I invested all of it in real estate, which I had thought was "safe."

I will never forget the day when my wife and I sold our house. We went to the title company to close, and it covered the millions of dollars of debt. We hugged each other and repeatedly said to each other, "Oh my God, we are out of debt." But at that point, the only asset remaining was the $157,000 of cash value in my life insurance policy. We moved into a rental property with the family.

Because I short-sold my house, in order to purchase another home and leverage the lower home prices and mortgage rates, my father was kind enough to co-sign with me. But I procured the down payment from my remaining asset. How?

In order to have the down payment to purchase my house, I borrowed against the cash value of the life insurance policy. I then paid that loan back over the five years that I was living in the home, and making improvements to the home. There was another opportunity to buy another home, which was a repossession. To seize this opportunity, I again borrowed against the life insurance policy's cash value as my down payment and secured a mortgage for the remainder.

I was then able to decide whether to sell my first home or use it as a rental property. I sold that house, which allowed me to pay back the second loan to the policy. I have repeated this process of borrowing against the policy to buy the next house, do some renovations, and sell for a profit and pay back the loan. This policy ended up being a lifeline and an alternate way of leveraging real estate and moving my wealth forward.

This is a story of cash and capital. In a life insurance policy, you will never have less money than you had the year before. And it is not about rate of return – it is about access to capital and being able to borrow against the money to be able to take advantage of economic situations that you would never anticipate. This is one example of a guarantee of an asset. But what about income that could fluctuate?

7 |

HOW MUCH INCOME TO GUARANTEE: ALL, SOME, OR NONE

The only guarantees in life are death and taxes. While that may feel true, there are some things you can work on with your retirement strategy to guarantee income. But, how much guaranteed income is the right amount?

When you get to be in your later planning years of your life, between the ages of fifty and sixty-five, you may be in the stock market or have real estate, and it may end up becoming a lot of work. Many people think the time to acquire real estate is when they are older, but at some point, they will likely want to stop being managers of those types of assets.

As mentioned earlier in the book, I used our insurance policies in opportune ways at appropriate times in the housing market to borrow downpayments for real estate investments. At some point, however, the aggravation may be too great to outweigh the benefits of owning and managing real estate. You may then want to look for opportunities to be able to create new income streams.

I typically ask clients, "When planning for these income streams in your future, do you want all some or none of your income guaranteed?" And almost 99 percent of the time people will say they want some of the income guaranteed.

The reason is when you say the word guarantee, there's no risk implied. The risk is completely gone when you have a guaranteed contract. So many people start looking at creating these guarantees in the future, at maybe a 7, 8, or 9 percent rate of return, versus investing in the stock or bond market.

Annuities can be great products because they are designed to create income, and they offer guarantees by insurance companies, some of which have been in existence for hundreds of years. In terms of income planning products, annuities can coordinate well with other assets to create some guaranteed income streams.

Social Security is another form of guaranteed income, although there is a debate about whether this guaranteed income will be available to future generations. Combined with an annuity that can guarantee some level of income stream, the rest of your assets should work together to create maximum income, often higher than a 3 to 4 percent rate of return. You could plan to have approximately 50 percent of your income stream guaranteed.

For most people, the largest guaranteed income stream will come from Social Security. In fact, there are statistics that show that Social Security will be the largest income stream that retirees will rely on for living expenses. It is imperative during your lifetime that you save money in other asset types such as IRAs, Roth IRAs, 401(k) plans, annuities, insurance, etc. to create additional sources of income in case these benefits get cut in the future.

What about the people who badmouth annuities? One of my clients has adult children. One of the children has an advisor, and the advisor has said not to use annuities because of some outdated reasoning.

The first is the supposed high commission. While it's true that commissions and fees were very high in the past, especially for variable annuities, many are currently half of what they were. In fact, there are new regulations around commissions, fiduciary duty and the suitability of annuities that have been enacted to protect consumers.

Next is the concern about a small rate of return. This is reflected in a fixed annuity, which might have a lower rate of return but also is guaranteed with a zero percent chance of losing money in the market based on the strength of the insurance company offering it. But even those rates are reasonable, especially today. A fixed annuity works much like a bank CD but may offer a better rate.

In fact, this book is written during a period of higher interest rates, which has made annuities become increasingly attractive. During times with higher interest rates, you can lock in higher guarantees, and depending on how the annuity is structured, there is an opportunity to accumulate more money to offset periods of lower interest rates.

There are a couple of things to consider when it comes to annuities. One is that annuities are contracts between you and an insurance company. They are not liquid and most have surrender periods if you want out.

It's important to understand how long this surrender period lasts per your specific annuity contract terms— eight, ten, twelve or fifteen years. It's also why you want to have enough money in an emergency fund to cover unexpected expenses so you don't have to cancel an annuity and take a loss during its surrender period.

You don't want to have all of your money in an annuity—in fact, most insurance companies won't allow it. You want to have the right amount to help you generate the appropriate amount of retirement income for your lifestyle in combination with Social Security and other guaranteed income streams. It's a long-term strategy.

In addition to guaranteed income, an annuity such as a fixed indexed annuity (FIA) offers the opportunity for growth based on an index like the S&P 500. While not actually invested in the stock market, the index serves as a benchmark the insurance company uses for crediting your FIA policy. But best of all, although you have the chance for growth, an FIA also comes with zero-guarantee floor. This means that even if the benchmark index is losing money, your policy will never be credited less than zero—so your FIA is not subject to market risk.

As an example, let's say you have a $100,000 annuity which offers annual crediting, and receive a rate of return of 5 percent. That means the annuity's value at the end of year one is $105,000. The next year, if the market dives, the index might have a rate of return of -7 percent. Yet at the end of year two, your annuity would still be worth $105,000.

Many FIA policies offer some amount of growth no matter what the index is doing. Some offer uncapped growth, while some come with caps or participation rates. Some provide guarantee lifetime income no matter how long you live. Each annuity contract is very different—some even come with additional features, or features that can be added as an annuity contract "rider" for an additional cost. For instance, you could even have long-term care coverage as part of your particular annuity.

Do not listen to naysayers stuck in the past. Look instead at what is in the present by investigating annuities for yourself. Things have changed, from compliance to benefits, because of higher interest rates and improved policy designs. There may be a great opportunity for people to address multiple needs with an annuity as part of their retirement plan.

If you have not considered annuities in this new light, this would be a good time to explore this option.

8 |

LOVE THOSE EMPLOYER GROUP BENEFITSE

Besides money, you may feel there are not a lot of tangible benefits when it comes to working. Employees often overlook the group benefits that employers provide, which can be a goldmine if leverage appropriately. Let's talk about what to love and hate when it comes to employer group benefits.

The best part of employer group benefits is you do not have to pay much money, if at all, for the benefits, with the exception of health insurance. Let's focus on supplementary group benefits that are offered or are free. You work for a company, and they provide you with disability and life insurance, and you pay a small amount for this benefit. They also provide short-term disability insurance, and sometimes supplemental voluntary benefits like Aflac, at a cost paid by the employee.

These three benefits (short-term disability, long-term disability and life insurance) are ones that you can get from your employer. These are great things to have, and they are sometimes free or at little expense. But there are things lacking.

When you get into detail about your disability insurance, if it is employer paid, it's a taxable event if you receive it. Let's say you are covered for 60 percent of your income up to $10,000 a month. That amount can become taxable to you when you receive it. If both you and your employer have paid the premiums for the plan, only the amount you receive for your disability that's due to your employer's payments is reported as income. If you are in the 30 percent tax bracket, you are only netting $7,000 a month. Is that enough money to pay for your expenses?

Today, many employers are helping employees with the income tax burden on the disability insurance by including the cost of the payroll tax in their paycheck to create tax-free disability insurance benefits.

One of the things that I suggest is to add a supplemental individual benefit to fill the gap. This is because group benefits are not written to pay you long-term. Depending on your occupation, some of the group benefits will only be written for two years with a definition of what you are engaged in at the time you become disabled. After two years it could be anything you are trained for by education and experience. I recommend investigating an individual noncancelable guaranteed renewable supplemental insurance policy and its specific terms.

Short-term disability cannot be purchased on an individual basis, which makes it one of the best benefits to have from an employer. Again, make sure the group benefit is enough for your age and living situation. The reason why you work at a job is to get benefits. It makes sense to understand how these benefits work. Whether you are paying for them or not, they could be benefits to leverage.

When an employer offers life insurance as a benefit to their employees, and it is paid for, most often it is term life insurance. This is different than permanent life insurance but plays a part in the overall strategy to maximize income.

Additional life insurance could be less expensive outside of these group benefits but may require underwriting. If you are healthy, it may be worth the time to explore this option.

One thing to consider: when purchasing term life insurance with your employer, the cost normally goes up in five-year increments. However, leveraging term life insurance, especially if you do not have other options, can provide temporary protection for your family that could become extremely necessary should they unexpectedly lose you.

Any number of health-related or unforeseen events could happen to any of us at any time. This includes needing long-term care, and that prospect is not something to avoid, it is something to plan ahead for.

9 |

LONG-TERM CARE IS NOT SOMETHING TO IGNORE

What are your plans for your later years, especially when you may need assistance with long-term care? Are you financially ready to supply those necessary resources, or is your family ready to sacrifice time and energy to supply care?

The traditional long-term care product that has been around for over forty years is no longer a great choice in most cases. When I started in this business, traditional long-term care insurance was being sold and it was a new product. The only way that someone could purchase a long-term care policy was if a policy was bought on both the husband and wife from an insurance carrier. Typically, this would require two separate policies. Today there are carriers that will write one policy for both husband and wife.

Over the last forty years, insurance carriers have increased premiums, often at the time of life when policyholders would most likely need long-term care. Long-term care policies are like health insurance and the carrier can increase premiums every year, unlike many disability policies. Because of this, long-term care policies are often very expensive, and as LTC policy holders reach age 65 or older, they may have to cancel or reduce benefits in order to afford the premiums.

There is another way to add long-term care coverage as part of your retirement strategy: asset-based long-term care. There are two ways this can be used.

In the first, if you never use it, the payout will go to your estate or your beneficiaries, whoever you choose. In the second, you can decide to cancel it, and you will receive a portion of your money back, depending on when you cancel it. And if you use it, it pays income directly to the caregiver or facility for the rest of your life. This is called a reimbursement policy. There are also policies that will pay you directly called indemnity policies.

That's what I call the win-win-win. And bonus: the premiums are locked so you will not need to worry about a rate increase. You can pay the premium in one lump sum, pay over the rest of your life, or five, ten, or twenty years. You can also use your IRA or 401(k) required distribution or RMD—which kicks in starting at age 73—to pay the premium as well, assuming you don't need the money for retirement income or other expenses.

The newest options for long-term care insurance have become better and more diverse than they ever have been, and it is a great time to explore these types of products.

If you have current coverage, be sure to review your policy. Many of these policies have limitations on how long the benefits will be paid for. Healthcare costs will continue to rise and can be the number one expense that can deplete your retirement nest egg—or your entire estate if you have to qualify for Medicaid. Having a long-term care policy can be a life saver.

10 |

MAKING YOUR LIST AND CHECKING IT TWICE

In the words of music great Duke Ellington, "A goal is a dream with a finish line."

There are many ways to successfully reach the retirement finish line. Having a list and knowing your options can help you consider things that might be easily overlooked.

You may not be thinking about checklists that include items like Social Security and Medicare, but these are critical when looking at a strong retirement plan.

The LEAP System is a model I have studied throughout my career. One of the critical components of the LEAP System is Social Security. Why is there a component specifically for Social Security? Because many people do not check their Social Security statements.

More times than not, there is a miscalculation in your Social Security benefits because the correct taxes or the correct income were not used. One of the most important annual tasks you can do is check how much money has been declared as income and what your Social Security benefit is. This can help ensure that there are no mistakes.

Another thing not fully understood with Social Security is that if you have a non-working spouse, the benefit for the non-working spouse is 50 percent of the working spouse's benefit. In other words, even if you are a non-working spouse and you have not paid into Social Security, you can still get 50 percent of your husband's benefit when you both go on Social Security.

What if you become divorced? You are also entitled to part of your ex-spouse's Social Security benefit if you were married for ten years or more. In some states, you may be able to get both the 50 percent of your current spouse's benefits as well as a portion of your ex-spouse's benefits.

If your spouse dies, many people think that they will continue to get their spouse's Social Security benefits, but that is not the case. The higher of the two is continued to be paid to the surviving spouse. That is important for planning.

As mentioned earlier, there is a statistic that says that 40 percent or more of people will only have Social Security benefits as their income in retirement because they failed to plan. It is important to go to ssa.gov to look into everything that you are entitled to with Social Security.

If you have children that are less than eighteen years old and your spouse passes away, your children are entitled to Social Security benefit until they turn eighteen. That money must be utilized for that child and is subject to auditing.

Social Security, unfortunately, has become the largest form of retirement income stream that we currently have in the U.S. Be sure to learn how those income streams from the government work. You can plan and make sure you have what you are entitled to, since you have been paying into it your entire life.

Keep this on your checklist and make sure you monitor your Social Security benefit. If you do not do so, you may be leaving money on the table.

11 |
YOUR FIVE WORST FINANCIAL ENEMIES

What is the biggest fear you have when it comes to losing your savings for retirement?

What if I told you that there are at least five wealth eroding factors that should be on your radar: government taxes, inflation, planned obsolescence items, technology expenses, and interest rates?

Let's start with taxes. Our taxes are going to go up, go down, and even go sideways. Every person that I talk to says taxes are going to go up in the future, and why are they going to go up in the future? If you look at the national debt that is accumulating right now, it is almost impossible to stop that number from going up.

The only way that the U.S. government is going to get that debt down is to increase taxes. Most people think that their taxes only consist of federal and state income taxes, but there are also payroll taxes. If you are in the 15 or 20 percent tax bracket, add another 7.5 percent for payroll taxes.

Let's think about other taxes that you may not have considered that are going to go up as well.

If you own a home and you look at your real estate taxes, it is probably those taxes will go up. Think about sales tax as well. If you live in a state where there is sales tax, have you seen your sales tax go up?

When you look at the taxes in the future, you cannot just look at your federal and state income taxes. Based on your income, you are most likely going to be taxed on Social Security benefits. There are several wealth-eroding factors to consider.

You are going to be buying goods and services that will include sales taxes, and you are going to live in your house until you downsize and there will be real estate taxes to pay. The next thing to think about with wealth-eroding factors is inflation. We have seen inflationary numbers up above 7 to 8 percent recently.

Compare inflation to oranges that are left on your tree from last season, and the older oranges have been eaten by microscopic organisms. That is inflation. It slowly erodes your wealth if you are not careful.

That is the whole reason for workers that are on strike from the United Auto Workers and the strikes by writers and the actors in the last few years. Inflation has increased so high that the auto workers, for example, wanted a 40 percent pay increase.

You are trying to retire and put money away to save for your future. You are preparing for retirement. Without question, you are going to have to spend money.

For example, I have a client that sold their house and followed their dream, which was to buy a RV and travel around the United States. Well, the RV is constantly breaking down. They need money to fix the RV.

The same can be said for owning a home. You may need a new roof, or an air conditioning unit. You need to consider planned obsolescence, otherwise known as wealth eroding.

Let's move onto technology. Do you have the same cell phone from ten years ago? Do you have the same computer from ten years ago? Technology is our best friend and our biggest enemy for future expenses. Most technology makes items we need more expensive. Even cars are more expensive because of technology.

You have to use technology services from experts. Technological change is something that is always going to be around and can easily be wealth eroding.

Last is rising interest rates. How do rising interest rates affect you? With a rising period of inflation, you will always see the government increasing rates in order to try to stop the increased inflationary costs, which increases interest rates in money markets, savings and CDs.

Sounds great, right? Think about whether you want to sell your house and buy a new one. When the Fed starts raising rates, that is going to affect our ability to borrow money, including securing a mortgage.

Interest rates can work to your benefit with savings during a rising period of those rates. But if you need capital, it is a huge cost that could erode your wealth. And if you are a business owner, there is even more to consider.

Because business owners are likely to leverage debt for some of their business expenses, this can affect profits and growth. For example, many business owners have a credit line to use versus their own business revenue. When interest rates go up for savings, they also go up for borrowing. And this can affect those business decisions.

There are things that cannot be avoided, like death and taxes, but understanding additional areas where wealth can be eroded can help with planning and strategy.

Speaking of taxes, the question becomes, is it better to pay tax on the seed or the harvest

12 |

DO YOU WANT TO PAY TAX ON THE SEED OR THE HARVEST

According to the Encyclopædia Britannica, the first record of farming is nearly 12,000 years ago. Even if you are not a farmer, you most likely understand planting seeds and collecting the harvest.

Let's talk about farmers in the Midwest. A farmer grows crops and those crops are going to develop into a harvest. That harvest can be compared to your wealth.

How does the government factor into that harvest? The government allows you to invest in pre-tax retirement plans, but you must remember that these are actually only tax-deferred. Eventually you will compound your wealth and by doing so, compound your taxes owed to the government.

What if you decided to pay taxes on the seed—your already-taxed money prior to putting it in a retirement portfolio—and compounding the interest, but then you did not have to pay taxes on the way out. Seems like you might have gotten away with something. Why would the government allow you to do this? Yet they do.

The government changed the regulations, now allowing you to delay your required minimum distributions (RMDs) on your taxable qualified plans like 401(k)s, increasing the age from seventy and a half to seventy-three. Why do you think the government is allowing you to do that? This is because you are compounding interest that is going to lead to higher taxable income when you start to take the annual distributions out. The new SECURE Act increased the age; it increases again to seventy-five in 2033.

There are ways to create a tax-free environment in your future, but you have to plan for that before you retire. Part of that, and the basis of this book, is planning for retirement income streams.

One of the options you have is called the Backdoor Roth IRA. This is where you can convert money held in taxable accounts into Roth non-taxable accounts, which means that you can create future tax-free income, or a portion of your money will be tax-free when you retire. Strict rules apply, and income taxes are paid in the years that you do any conversions on the converted amounts. It's best to work with an experienced advisor and accountant.

I advise my clients that are in their fifties and beyond to consider no longer putting any more money into a tax-deductible retirement plan and instead make a tax-free contribution (a Roth contribution).

If you have already put money into an IRA and acquired all the compound interest and the compound tax deferral, you may be concerned about future taxes. Backdoor Roth IRAs can come into play, where you start converting off portions of that traditional IRA into a Roth. All of the IRA can be converted by the time you retire so that you do not have any income taxes nor do you have required minimum distribution on that Roth IRA.

Like any financial planning, you should always consult with your tax advisor. You do not want to convert so much that you are put into a higher tax bracket. By planning now, you can set up part of your income stream to reduce taxes and remove some of the wealth eroding factors that catch retirees by surprise.

Since you are thinking more strategically, why not think like an institution that is a master at making money: a bank.

13 |
THINK LIKE A BANK

Have you ever thought of your finances like a bank does? Or for that matter, have you ever approached your finances as if you were your own bank?

Banks take out insurance policies on their employees called bank-owned life insurance (BOLI). If you look at banks and research banks, BOLI is the largest asset that banks own. Why is it the largest asset that banks own? Because banks do not lend their own money.

Instead, they leverage six to eight times the assets that they can lend to people in the form of different types of loans, whether it be credit cards, mortgages, car loans, home loans, et cetera. Well, if banks are able to leverage those assets, why do they use life insurance as the money that they count on their books, which is usually billions of dollars?

One of the important factors about whole life insurance is that it is guaranteed by insurance companies. Banks know with certainty how much money will be in those policies on a year-to-year basis based on the guarantees in the contract. The only moving part of the life insurance policy in a whole life insurance policy is the dividend, but they don't base the asset on dividends. They base it on the fact that they have a guaranteed contract.

Banks know exactly how much money each year will be there, which means that they can go to the Federal Reserve window and borrow eight times what they have on the books.

A bank never lends their own money. They lend other people's money, which would be the government. The government declares their money rate, which is called the federal funds rate, every month, and the banks leverage that as the funding for loans.

This is the tip of the bank-thinking iceberg.

Let's go back to my earlier story. If you recall, I had multiple policies which I owned that had cash value. If we go back to my story, what did I do with that cash value? I leveraged against it. I did not take money from it. The money still stayed "in the bank" so to speak.

Remember, if we are like the bank, what does the bank not do? The money used for lending does not come out of the bank. The banks go to the Federal Reserve window, and they pay interest to the Federal Reserve. The same thing can be said for a life insurance company.

You do not borrow from the policy; you borrow against the policy. The money still gets interest from the insurance company and dividends, in a specific and non-direct recognition way. And important to note: there are only certain companies that do it that way.

The idea is to borrow against your policies at a certain interest rate and pay the insurance company for an interest-only loan. Then you can use that capital to invest somewhere else. I did it with my house in the real estate crisis.

Think about this. Let's just say that you are younger and you think you are a great trader in the stock market, and you are statistically able to produce a rate of return of 10 percent.

Well, if it costs 5 percent to borrow against the life insurance cash value and I can make 10 percent on that money with certain strategies, you may think that is a 5 percent return. It is actually not.

It is a 100 percent return. That is called leverage. Remember when I said "math is not money and money is not math"? That is because you are leveraging other people's money, not your own.

This is what successful entrepreneurs do. If you think like a bank and use your life insurance policy as a starting point, it no longer becomes about the rate of return. It is about the ability to use leverage against an asset that no other asset can allow.

Some people erroneously believe having a home equity credit line can do the same thing. What they fail to realize is that you could spend all your home equity credit line, and if the banks decide to freeze that money, like they did in my story, then you are locked out. Using cash value of a life insurance policy is thinking and acting like a bank. Even during the Great Depression, it was the only place that people didn't experience a loss of their money.

You are starting to think like a bank. The next step in the evolution is to be your own bank. Scandalous or ingenious?

14 |
BE YOUR OWN BANK

The worst saying of all time is this: "You have to spend money to make money."

What would be more accurate is this: "You have to leverage money to make money."

Leveraging money means you are going to be like a bank. And to be like a bank, you are going to lend to yourself. Let's consider an example of being like a bank.

Let's take another example and instead consider purchasing a car. Current interest rates on cars are incredibly high, anywhere from 7 to 8 percent. But, considering the same example as above, I can buy a $50,000 car and borrow against my cash value at 5 percent.

The cash value is still going to grow with dividends and interest, whether the money is in the policy or not. That's a great place to go for the money. And I can pay off the loan sooner if I have the cash flow.

If I get into trouble, because it is an interest-only loan, I can pay the minimum interest. However, I always want to pay the loan back. I want to pay more than the loan interest rate back so I can redeploy that money again.

You can think of this strategy as acquiring an asset and using the asset income to pay yourself back. If you are buying a car, that is a depreciated asset. However, you would be utilizing it as a strategy during periods of high interest.

People also use this strategy to send children to college, pay for a child's wedding, help a child out with a first home purchase. You can even have your child have their own insurance policy money to put in. Instead of borrowing for college, they can also leverage the cash value.

When you send your kids to college and pay for college out of your own money, it is also considered to be an opportunity cost. One of the things that people never take into consideration is the opportunity cost.

In almost all financial decisions, you must consider the opportunity cost. If you send your kids to college using your own money, you just created one. You have to take money from somewhere that was making money to do that. If I take it from an insurance policy and pay it back, it is no longer an opportunity cost.

You can always pay yourself back. As was stated before, this is thinking, and acting, like a bank. Banks, for the most part, stay solvent well beyond us mere mortals.

The housing crisis and current mortgage interest rates may make you feel that real estate investment is no longer a good idea. Let me help set the record straight.

15 |
PURCHASE A RENTAL PROPERTY

As the American humorist Will Rogers once said, "Don't wait to buy real estate, buy real estate and wait."

One of the fastest ways to increase wealth is to have someone else pay your loan while your investment continues to grow in value. This is essentially what happens when you have a rental property. Your tenant pays the mortgage via the rent payment, and the asset also continues to increase in value.

I have a calculator that calculates the rate of return on real estate. The way I teach people to buy real estate is to accumulate their down payment through a life insurance policy and borrow against the cash value for the down payment.

By doing that, it increases the rate of return on the overall plan. Not only are you still making interest on your life insurance cash values through non-direct recognition of dividends, but the policy also doesn't recognize whether the money is in or out of it in order to pay dividends.

In other words, if the insurance company sends the money to the client, the client can use that money as a down payment for a rental property. The client then pays back the money to the policy. The money is now available to borrow against for another property, which can be put into another potential rental property.

If the rental property cash flows, you can pay yourself back through the cashflow of the rental property. I always recommend using loans or mortgages to buy properties because of the compound tax deduction of the interest.

Interest is tax deductible on an investment property, and an investment property is depreciated, usually over twenty-seven years. Therefore, the tax benefits are substantial. But what people miss when calculating rates of return is you can compound that tax benefit if you were to invest that money somewhere else.

This allows a rate of return on a rate of return, whether it produces cashflow or not on the property. Rental properties alone, without any cashflow, are usually going to grow in value.

An insurance company sends a check to you. You pay the insurance company back, including a small amount of interest per policy terms (currently at 5 percent). You can then pay more or just pay the interest only, and you have two investments making money.

In short, per IRS guidelines, you can overfund the life insurance policy to give you the money to borrow from it (Of course, certain restrictions apply).

Suppose I have $100,000 of cash value in my policies. I have identified an investment property that I would like to buy. The property is on the market for $400,000 and my plan is to use the property as a rental. But I need a down payment.

Now where do I get the money for the down payment? I could liquidate an investment or take it from savings because I need $80,000 as a down payment. Alternatively, I can go to my insurance company and it quotes a 5 percent rate on an $80,000 loan against my policy cash value. The loan is an interest-only loan and at 5 percent of $80,000 equates to $4,000 a year, or $333.33 a month.

I am required to pay the interest back on the insurance policy loan every year. Why would I borrow against my cash value in my life insurance policy versus liquidating an investment or using cash? The answer is because of opportunity cost. If you liquidate you are going to lose interest, dividends, or investment gains. The opportunity cost is the highest rate of return that you are earning on your investments minus taxes.

Do you have opportunity costs by borrowing against your life insurance? The answer is no, because you are still earning interest and dividends on the borrowed funds.

I purchase the rental property by acquiring a thirty-year conventional mortgage for $320,000. The rental property will produce $3,000 a month of rental income, or $36,000 a year. Now I am able to pay the interest from my down payment loan and pay my monthly mortgage, depending on the interest rate I received.

If the mortgage rate is 6.5%, then the monthly payments on a thirty-year loan will be $2022.62 per month. You have a positive cash flow of almost

$1000, to cover taxes, insurance and interest payment to the insurance company. My asset will make money and hopefully continue to increase in equity.

Here is another example of this concept in action. Greg and Sue, in order to purchase their first house, borrowed against the cash value of their life insurance policy. They paid that loan back over five years while living in the house and making improvements to it (and increasing the overall value). Another opportunity presented itself, to purchase another home that they would move into.

They were able to, first, borrow again against the life insurance policy for the downpayment, which was 20 percent of the negotiated price and they obtained a mortgage for the remainder.

They then took the first home and made it a rental property, since it was their starter home. They then paid back the loan from the life insurance policy, and they now have two properties: one that is their primary residence and one that provides income.

You could argue that the personal residence has no rate of return. But there is a way calculate the rate of return. If you were to rent that house instead of purchasing, it would cost you X amount of dollars per month. If you didn't own it, you would be renting it. That monthly rental fee would be the rate of return on your primary property. A personal residence should be part of your overall balance sheet.

I believe owning a personal residence is the best investment that any person, young or old, could ever make. It is the start of the best investment that you invest in yourself. My motto is: invest in your home before you invest in any rental properties.

Let's dive deeper into borrowing against your insurance policy cash value. What does that really mean, and why does that strategy work?

16 |

BORROW AGAINST CASH VALUE

There is famous fatherly advice in William Shakespeare's play, Hamlet. The character Polonius counsels his son Laertes before he embarks on his visit to Paris. He says, "Neither a borrower nor a lender be."

Sorry Polonius, I have to disagree with you there.

When people hear the term borrow it can cause a myriad of thoughts.. Who am I borrowing from? What will be the cost of borrowing? Am I better off saving rather than borrowing? Not all borrowing is bad – there is good debt. The key is to know when borrowing works to increase your retirement wealth. Borrowing against the cash value of your life insurance policy is a borrowing methodology that can work.

Let's address the first misnomer. When you borrow against the cash value of your life insurance policy, it doesn't actually come from the cash value. Let's view this in an example. You have a $100,000 in cash value in your policy and you want to use that money to invest. You are not borrowing from it because doesn't leave the policy.

It stays in the policy and the insurance company gives you the money. The reason why they do these loans is because it is the best loan they can have on the books. The loan is collateralized by the cash value that is in the policy. In a non-direct recognition company, the company doesn't act like the money is out of the policy.

In essence, the money stays in the policy and actually comes from the insurance company. They file a collateral assignment against your personal note that you take from the insurance company. You pay a small interest, and you pay the loan back like you would pay back any loan that you would have.

As you saw in the previous chapter, I recommend using your life insurance policy cash value for real estate. You could also use your cash value when you need a cash buffer. Fast forward to retirement - you have accumulated cash value in your policy and you are taking withdrawals from your existing assets.

The policy's cash value is what we call a non-correlated asset to the stock or bond market. Therefore, because it's non-correlated and guaranteed, then the only moving part is the dividend. Once the dividend is paid by an insurance company, it becomes part of the guarantee.

When you are withdrawing money from an account as a retiree, the money that you borrow against the account in retirement doesn't necessarily have to be paid back. When you start taking income from your assets, you never know what your rate of return is going to be until the end of the year.

If you had a loss in the stock market, it's best to hold off taking money from there and use the non-correlated asset of cash value of your life insurance. This can be used as a buffer to give those investments time to grow back. This helps eliminate a permanent loss. It's easier for the money to grow back when you don't withdraw from it when it's down. You will need to analyze this on a year-to-year basis.

I think for major expenses, such as a wedding for your child or a car purchase, can also be when you would use your insurance policy for a loan you pay back. This is where you need to consider the opportunity cost.

Most people do not calculate opportunity costs in their retirement plan. An opportunity cost, by definition, is the highest rate of return on your money net of taxes on your model or in your portfolio.

If your highest rate of return in your 401(k) plan is 9 percent, when you take out that money and pay taxes, it may be net 7 percent. That's the opportunity cost – what you take from yourself and give to somebody else, including Uncle Sam.

There are certain opportunity costs you cannot avoid. Those are considered to be costs because you will never get that money back. In a situation where you give money to your kids for college or for a wedding, it is best to use your insurance policy and pay yourself back. This will help you avoid opportunity cost on your money for your retirement.

17 |
RETIRE WITH A VOLATILITY BUFFER

A 2023 survey found that sixty-one percent of Americans are more afraid of running out of money in old age than of dying itself. Life insurance giant Allianz, which conducted the survey, found the result "remarkable," but actually, it makes sense.

There is volatility in the financial market, and there is no way around it. Before you start to panic, financial advisors have taken this into account. A good financial advisor will speak to you about adding a volatility buffer to your retirement plan. While we cannot eliminate volatility altogether, we can greatly reduce the impact.

As things affect how far your money will go, such as inflation, rate of return on investment, or tax-rate changes, you may find yourself not having enough money to cover future retirement expenses.

To have the money to pay your bills, you may decide to take higher withdrawals from your accumulated assets held in accounts correlated to the stock market. If, after some years, your assets didn't earn enough to cover what you were planning to pull out (because you cannot predict future returns), you would need the ability to withdraw your income from a different asset–one that is uncorrelated to the stock market.

Yes, we are talking about life insurance, again. However, life insurance provides a variety of nets and buffers that can help protect your future asset value. Let's assume you have done well and have $1 million in your 401(k).

In Scenario A, you could be pulling 100 percent of your money out of your retirement plan or 401(k) at a low withdrawal rate, let's use 3.5 percent as an example. That means a low withdraw amount over a long period of time, so you need to continue to pinch your pennies. That sounds like a depressing retirement plan, especially after amassing such a large 401(k).

To increase your cash flow, let's say you decided to increase the withdraw rate. Obviously, you are going to have less money in your 401(k) if you take higher withdrawals. You could use withdrawals to fund life insurance. For example, instead of having $1 million, you would have $750,000 and use $250,000 to purchase life insurance with a death benefit and cash value.

When you are reviewing your 401(k)'s ability to provide retirement income, you are often looking at an average rate of return, not a constant year-over-year rate. That means that in some years, you could have a high rate of return and in others, a negative return (meaning your asset value goes down). The sequencing of the rates of return affects the sustainability of your withdraw plan.

When you take out money during a year that has a negative return, in order to make up the difference, you will need to have a much higher positive rate of return to stay on track because you have a permanent loss. There will be a need to make up the loss of the asset to be back to the proper value levels. You won't know what that particular year's rate of return is until the year is over.

You can buffer this volatility with a withdraw from the life insurance policy, which is not correlated to the economy or stock market. This causes the rate of return to be fixed. When you see the 401(k) has recovered, you are good to go back to withdrawing from the 401(k) plan.

If you work with your financial advisor to look at the different withdraw rates, to reduce the probability of running out of money, the withdraw has to be conservative (around 3 percent or less). This is because there is volatility in the market and a reduction in the length of time you have to recover that loss. This information is based on thousands of simulations over forty years in a variety of market sectors.

When you add the volatility buffer, you have more room to withdraw and less consideration of market changes when you go to use those funds. The buffer, as you use it for more years during your retirement, adds more stability to your retirement plan.

When you are living through your retirement years, do you really want to be saddled with fear that your money could run out? What if, in order to make it to the end of retirement, you felt you had to come out of retirement to bring in extra cash?

While you never can guarantee that you will have enough money, by adding in a volatility buffer, you are increasing your chances of having enough money to make it to the end of retirement in a lifestyle that is comfortable and enjoyable – because that is what retirement should be about.

THE IMPACT OF MARKET VOLATILITY AND COMPARING AN AVERAGE RATE OF RETURN TO AN ACTUAL RETURN STRATEGY.

Recouping Big Losses Is Tough

The math of percentages shows that as losses get larger, the return necessary to recover to break-even increases at a much faster rate. A loss of 10 percent necessitates an 11 percent gain to recover. Increase that loss to 25 percent and it takes 33 percent gain to get back to break-even. A 50 percent loss requires a 100 percent gain to recover and an 80 percent loss necessitates 500 percent in gains to get back to where the investment value started. Below is an example of why it is worth caring about market losses:

Accumulation Portfolio	
No Withdrawal	
Loss	Break Even
-5%	+5.26%
-10%	+11.11%
-20%	+25%
-30%	+43%
-40%	+67%
-50%	+100%
-60%	+150%
-70%	+233.3%
-80%	+400%
-90%	+900%

Distribution Portfolio			
Withdrawal Rate			
Loss	4%	6%	8%
-5%	+14.68%	+20.1%	+26%
-10%	+21.5%	+27.3%	+33.7%
-20%	+37.4%	+44.5%	+52.5%
-30%	+58.5%	+67.5%	+77.4%
-40%	+86.6%	+98.5%	+111.9%
-50%	+127.3%	+145%	+163.3%
-60%	+190.8%	+217%	+247.5%
-70%	+303.5%	+351%	+410.5%
-80%	+558%	+682%	+862%
-90%	+1686%	+2845%	+8234%

How Much Risk Do You Need to Take?

Does high risk always equal high return? Historically this has not always been the case. High risk may produce high returns, but the contrary is just as true: high risk may also equal big losses and increased volatility.

Consistency Matters

Our industry uses many terms that end up being more confusing than helpful for clients.. Internal rate of return, time weighted rate of return, actual return, average rate of return, and many more. One rate of return many are familiar with is the average rate of return. While this is an important metric, it rarely tells the full story when analyzing account performance. Below is a table that shows how a person can average a 5% rate of return, but only actually have a 2.36% rate of return:

Average Return: 5.00%			Actual Return: 2.36%		
Year	Beg. Of Year Acct. Value	Earnings Rate	Annual Cash Flow	Interest Earnings	End of Year Acct. Value
1	100,000	30.00%		30,000	130,000
2	130,000	(25.00%)		(32,500)	97,500
3	97,500	10.00%		9,750	107,250

Having big returns and big losses can create large divergences between the average rate of return commonly talked about and actual rates of return. This is why consistency matters when speaking about returns. Not only is it difficult to recuperate from large losses (exacerbated when accounts and portfolios are providing income) as illustrated above, consistency in returns closes the gap between average and actual rates of returns.

18 |
COVERED ASSET MOVE

Do you remember the nightmare market crash in the early 2000's? Many people, who had been set to retire in a couple of years, had 40 percent or more of their 401(k) investment disappear overnight.

As we plan for the retirement years, having a portion of our money guaranteed would help all of us sleep a little better.

A covered asset move looks at making a portion of your retirement money guaranteed. You cannot have all of your retirement money guaranteed, but it would be great to have some guaranteed, right?

What constitutes a guaranteed income stream? One form of guaranteed income is an annuity stream of income backed by an insurance company. When choosing an annuity, you can choose one that has a lifetime guaranteed income stream. If you choose this type of annuity, you are making an irrevocable decision.

This is similar to those who take money from a pension plan from a government or a municipal institution. You can choose either Option A, which provides payments for your life, or Option B, which includes rights of survivorship paid to a spouse. With this sort of choice also offered by an annuity, you can set up your own personal pension.

What compares most closely with the pension form of defined benefit plan is a single premium immediate annuity. Let's take, for example, that you have an annuity, but without life insurance. Also say, for the sake of argument, that you are married. If you pass away prior to your spouse, you could choose to go with Option B, which provides a much lower payment. Otherwise, your spouse loses the income stream for the rest of her/his life.

What if your spouse predeceases you? You cannot have a do-over and choose Option A. A smarter way might be to cover that asset or set up a covered asset move with life insurance.

If you have $500,000 of life insurance and a retirement plan with this annuity, you have the option to take a life-only annuity payment through a single premium immediate annuity. If you die prematurely, your spouse will get the life insurance instead of that annuity asset. He/she is still covered.

In other words, utilizing life insurance allows you to maximize your pension. This is also called pension maximation. A life insurance policy gives you permission to make this decision in the event of an early or untimely death. You can create the same concept with other assets. You can exchange all or some of the asset for a single premium immediate annuity (SPIA).

Many times, those assets are in qualified plans like IRAs or 401(k)s. You would be giving your spouse a tax-free death benefit versus a tax-free spousal rollover, which is taxable upon taking the money out. The only thing your spouse could do is leave it to one of your children (if you have children) upon his or her death. However, your children would have to pay taxes out in a beneficiary IRA over ten years.

If you do the covered asset move using life insurance and you predecease your spouse and you leave that life insurance policy, that cash can be invested and income taken from it.

That also means it can grow when you pass on. Those assets get a step-up in basis from the IRS. Therefore, there is no estate or income tax if the monetary value is under a certain estate tax level.

This is an area that people frequently get wrong–understanding when beneficiaries have to pay taxes. For example, one of my clients thought her children had to pay taxes on a non-qualified asset when she died.

If you do a covered asset move and you buy life insurance, you are eligible to take Option A either on your pension or another guaranteed income source that you can create through a single premium annuity while still providing rights of survivorship.

Reverse mortgages can be another opportunity for people who are retired. You can prevent being kicked out of your house and create additional income by either not having to pay your mortgage payment anymore, or get an income or take a credit line out that you could start using and never have to pay back.

When you and/or your spouse die, the beneficiaries can sell the house. Any additional equity after the reverse mortgage is paid goes to the beneficiaries, which is typically factored in so the house will still have equity. You will able to have a better lifestyle in your retirement years and not have to sell your house to do so.

Reverse mortgages also work for people that haven't planned very well, but still want to maintain some of their lifestyle. This creates an asset for an income stream down the road. If you die prematurely, your spouse will still be able to continue to live there and either not have a mortgage payment or be able to take income from it on a tax-free basis because it's considered a loan.

All of these strategies are more than simple arithmetic. You need an expert to help you analyze these options. There is too much at stake to try to figure everything out yourself. You can, and should, educate yourself, but have a coach in retirement that is a fiduciary to go through the options with you to help you make the best choice.

This is an investment that does not have to be price-prohibitive. There are a variety of ways that advisors get paid. But the key is to work with someone who can help you make sense of the options and help you navigate the choices. This is your retirement future—one that can be strong and allow you to maintain your lifestyle. Or it could be a series of missed opportunities that derail all of your hard work and earnings.

A key area for the creation of a strong future is understanding how to work a paydown strategy.

19 |
PAYDOWN STRATEGY

What if you could amp up your retirement into a cashflow powerhouse? Part of that powerhouse should be leveraging paydown strategies in your plan.

There is no better way to say this: paydown strategies are awesome. This is a prime example of leveraging a financial advisor, since he or she will have access to tools and be able to navigate these complicated sequencing of rates of return in retirement to take income and live a comfortable lifestyle.

Everything in this book is about maximizing income. A paydown strategy helps with achieving that maximum income. Let's look at an example.

Amy retires with a million dollars, and decides to take out a high sustainable withdrawal rate of 4 percent, or $40,000 a year. For the sake of this example, let's not worry about taxes or inflation.

Amy takes that $40,000 per year, which is slightly lower than the 5 percent interest she is receiving from the account. She has a tiny bit of growth because she is doing an interest-only withdraw. She decides to take that $1 million down to zero over a twenty-year period. She retired at sixty-five and plans on using that money to eighty-five, when she expects the account to be down to zero.

While she is paying it down, hopefully she is using some of the principles in this book. Her tax liability will be less. The only problem is if she lives beyond eighty-five years old, she could run out of money.

I have said it before, and I will say it again: part of your playbook should include purchasing this non-correlated asset called life insurance. The exponential curve for rate of return on life insurance is huge between sixty-five and eighty-five. That twenty-year period is a rocket because that is when dividends kick in due to the cash available.

Amy may have $600,000 to $800,000 of cash value in that life insurance policy that she could use. She can pull all that money out tax-free. She now has two assets to help her in her retirement versus just one asset.

There is a focus today on micro-economically managing one asset to get some type of lifestyle out of it. Management can be much easier with a backup, and I believe that should be permanent life insurance.

Amy may run out of money, but she can tap into the cash value of the life insurance at eighty-five years old and withdraw more money because there are no taxes on the withdrawals.

Look at the life insurance cash value like a reverse mortgage. There will always be a death benefit, meaning you have an asset to leave to a beneficiary. You will still be able to use the cash value for yourself.

The other benefit is there are no taxes on the cash value unless you surrender it. It provides tax-free income, which means you need less of a withdraw to have the same net amount. That is one way to make your money work better for you.

20 |
THE MAGNIFICENT SEVEN TO THE RESCUE

Sometimes a movie title is the perfect metaphor, such as "The Magnificent Seven."

"The Magnificent Seven" is a 1960 American Western film directed by John Sturges which stars Steve McQueen and Yul Brenner. The screenplay is a remake of Akira Kurosawa's 1954 Japanese film "Seven Samurai." A movie with that same title was released in 2016, directed by Antoine Fuqua and starring Denzel Washington and Chris Pratt.

When you are preparing for your retirement years, there are seven assets that, if you have them, can increase the odds of your retirement being successful.

I nickname these The Magnificent Seven.

The first one is a 401(k) plan. Most people that work for a company have an established 401(k) plan. If you have a 401(k) account, my recommendation is to only put in whatever the maximum match is that the employer is putting in.

There are several reasons for that, and we have discussed those reasons. If you don't use a Roth IRA, you are going to pay tax on the entire harvest versus the seed that you started with.

To do this in the most efficient way, then you always want to get free money from your employer, no matter what form that free money comes in. With your 401(k), always put in the maximum that you can to maximize the match.

The second of The Magnificent Seven is real estate. There is no better investment than your own home. The reason is not only are you paying rent to yourself, you also have an asset that you can use in retirement.

Some people, as they approach retirement, say they are going to downsize. You get tax benefits when you sell your real estate because you have a marital tax exemption of $250,000 each. If you sell your home and you have $500,000 of profits, you don't have to pay taxes on that. Most people pay cash for their downsized house, but be aware that you have some tax benefits of selling it as your own personal residence.

If your house is already a perfect size and you don't want to leave it, research reverse mortgages as an option to enjoy and spend a portion of your wealth that you would have been spending on a mortgage payment. Reverse mortgages are currently protected by the government with specific rules. They are expensive, but they are an alternative way to live in your house and take joint income out for the rest of your lives and still leave the asset to your beneficiaries.

The third asset is your savings. Savings are an important asset. In most cases, you should have six months to one year of living expenses held in liquid savings accounts to cover emergencies or unexpected costs. If you are in retirement, have at least six months of savings or liquid assets that are put away on the side to take care of wealth eroding factors.

Life insurance is the fourth asset. It's the moat around your castle and allows you to do things with these other assets that you would never think about. It is the integration tool to create maximum income streams in your future.

Most people think that they don't need life insurance in retirement, because they've already replaced the value of the death benefit through other assets. During the discussion on Social Security, we reviewed how you are going to lose one of your Social Security income streams when you or your spouse dies.

That is a good reason to have life insurance. There are other examples in this "Max.Income.Playbook®" to use life insurance as a buffer to create maximum income streams or an exchange to create a pension or trade money for an income stream.

When you do that, you are making an irrevocable decision to trade your money for an income stream guaranteed for the rest of your life or both your life and your spouse. Life insurance would replace that asset if somebody was to die.

Suitable investments are incredibly important and are number five in the Magnificent Seven. I have seen seventy-seven-year-olds invested in aggressive mutual funds which are not suitable for the person and the amount of risk they should have. You always have to make sure that your investments are suitable for you because understanding markets is incredibly difficult. A good financial advisor can help you do more than navigate the markets, they can help you create a maximum income plan.

Advisors use a term called "risk tolerance." I call it "loss tolerance." How much tolerance do you have for losing your hard-earned money? An advisor may say, well, you really didn't lose any money because you haven't sold the position. However, in your mind, you just saw your money drop and your 401(k) plan went to a 201(k) plan. Did you put investments in places that were suitable for you?

Instead of risk tolerance, train your mind to loss tolerance and how much loss tolerance you have so that your investments are suitable, and you can handle that situation.

We work with business succession planning, which is number six. If you are an entrepreneur or business owner, you may have worked in your business your whole life and built it with the plan to sell it someday to create an income stream in retirement. Business assets are something that I deal with frequently with my designation as a Certified Family Business Specialist (CFBS) from The American College.

What is the most tax-advantaged way to do that? There are several strategies that you could use in retirement when you get to the point of selling your business or implementing your business succession plan. America is made up of small businesses and, while most want to have a succession plan, many don't because they haven't taken the time to create one. Your business is an important asset and the sooner you set up a succession plan, the better.

Particularly if you are in a service business, make sure that your clients know, in general terms, your succession plan as well. Your clients are your biggest assets in a business. You've worked all your life to build these relationships. You can keep those going perpetually for the rest of your life. Or you can go to a private equity company, and you will receive what is called an earnout, based on how much business sticks.

Let's talk about the last of The Magnificent Seven: the side business. As an example, one side business is buying and selling online. Some people don't want to have people come to their house and buy things. Instead of doing that, they hire someone and pay them a percentage of the profits.

There are benefits in setting up a side business. As a business owner, you can start writing off things that you never would think about. How much space in your house do you use to do this side business? What percentage of your car do you use for the side business? What about your mobile phone? What about your computer that you are using for your side business?

By setting up a side business, you are taking advantage of the tax code and becoming an entrepreneur. Some of these businesses that started out as a side business become a huge business.

This is not about taking advantage of deductions. This is actually creating a business that makes a profit for you. The laws of America allow you to do this because we are a nation of small businesses.

Apple started in a garage. Facebook started in a dorm room. Everybody can start a small business and let it grow to whatever you think it could be. I have known people that have started small businesses and have sold them for hundreds of millions of dollars.

I have a friend who is a TV repairman. He started a side business and people would say, "I don't want the old TV anymore. Can you haul it away?" He would say, "I'll haul it away for free." What he would then do is scavenge the valuable parts from it.

Then on eBay, people would say "Oh, I need this part." He has it and would then sell it. He is taking something that people think is worthless, yet he saw the hidden value. Through eBay, America's biggest garage sale, he was able to have a business.

Other people might have the skill of creating websites for people, and they would create websites on the side. All small businesses fill a valuable role, and that is what business is about. It's helping people get what they want, at a price they can afford, at a profit to you.

I recommend using the Magnificent Seven to help you shore up your retirement and put you into the Max.Income.Playbook®.

21 |
INTO THE RETIREMENT FUTURE

Sadly, there is no crystal ball to assess what obstacles could derail your retirement future. However, there are some trends to take into consideration.

Real Estate Market Pricing. With the changes in interest rates and the housing crisis aftermath, there is a perceived fluctuation in real estate value. However, this continues to be a key component in my Magnificent Seven.

While I am not an expert at real estate, I believe the most important part of purchasing real estate is the current financing rates, especially for investment property. Since I always recommend using leverage to purchase real estate, the focus should be on cash flow on the investment property.

You can still have a positive cash flow on your investment property, regardless of the increase in the real estate price. If you look at all of the tax benefits of owning real estate, even if it doesn't have positive cash flow right now, the property should still have positive returns.

Now keep in mind digital access to financial access.. You may have some valid concerns with digital fraud, identity theft and loss of financial assets due to cyber threats. There are ways to work with your financial advisor to be better protected.

First and most importantly, do not email your advisor for money withdrawals or changes. Always do this verbally. Also, use a two-factor authentication on your computer email. You can be sure there are people out there phishing all the time to access your email. Lastly, never write a check to your advisor. Only pay his/her advisory or directly to the custodian that holds your money.

You may have inflation concerns and are not sure what to expect in the future. It is hard to predict which sectors might be affected the most, or whether the inflation prices will come back down or stick to the higher level.

Plan on making sure your retirement income has inflationary factors built in because you can rest assured a car or cell phone, twenty years from now, will be more expensive.

When in doubt, err on the side of caution. Factor in inflation in your retirement plan with your financial advisor. If inflation does not happen at that level, you have given yourself a buffer.

Remote work is becoming more and more common. Financial experts have been asking if the continued rise of remote work will affect wage gains and how that might impact technology, real estate and business valuation.

As you know, more workers are demanding the flexibility of working from home. Wages have not increased at the inflationary pace and many workers are trying to reduce expenses by eliminating commuting costs, daycare and even additional work clothes and food expenses.

Because of this push for work-from-home, this will certainly impact residential property values and we will see prices go up. This also means commercial property values should start taking a hit, which could impact business valuation.

Then we factor in fintech innovation. There are ongoing developments in financial technology, including online banking and robo advisors. Robo advisors have been attempted and that technology has not had traction.

People want people to help them plan for their future. There are many advisors that have a ton of experience and are connected in financial circles that can really help the consumer. Sometimes "what you know" isn't as important as "who you know."

Financial professionals occupy a tried-and-true rule. Working with a financial advisor provides you with the guidance, expertise and financial tools to reach your retirement goals.

But not to just reach them. Because the objective is not to just climb to the top of the retirement mountain, it is also to make it safely down on the other side.

Making it to the top of your retirement journey is only half the story. The true test for a financial advisor is to help you safely make it through retirement. That is the easiest place to make mistakes not generating your retirement wealth but making decisions that erode it too quickly.

Saving money has been done for thousands of years with success. We have all heard of the schoolteacher that had millions of dollars saved when she passed on. But what were her "golden years" really like? Was she still worried and living a significantly reduced lifestyle? If she had a financial advisor, would she have been able to mark some things off her bucket list?

Maybe she could have taken that once-in-a-lifetime trip that never materialized because she didn't know if she could afford it. Maybe she could have assisted her children with purchasing their first new home without jeopardizing her retirement plan.

Perhaps her Social Security didn't cover as much as she had intended, and so she had to take on a part-time job to make ends meet. Or she had a real estate asset that she didn't leverage and left money on the opportunity table simply because it was not her area of expertise.

This book is titled "Max.Income.Playbook®" because there are various levels of success when it comes to playing the game of retirement. I personally want every client to have the maximum income they can in their retirement years, because they have worked hard to get to that point. No money left behind!

By having the right guide in place, you have the assistance and expertise to get through to the end of your retirement and enjoy the retirement you have worked so hard to achieve.

There is no reason for you to have to embark on this journey alone. Leverage the experts that have come before you and make your retirement the best it can be.

WORKS CITED

1. Robert Castiglione, LEAP: Lifetime Economic Acceleration Process, (City?, Castle Lion;, 2005).

2. U.S. Assisted Living Facility Market Size, Share & Trends Analysis Report 2020-2030, Grand View Research, https://www.grandviewresearch.com/industry-analysis/us-assisted-living-facility-market

3. Americans Facing a New Retirement Reality; Allianz Life Insurance Company of North America, May 31, 2023; https://www.allianzlife.com/about/newsroom/2023-press-releases/americans-facing-a-new-retirement-reality

4. Wealth Building Cornerstones. (n.d.). Retrieved Spring, 2024, from https://wbcornerstones.com/

5. Truth ConceptsTM Financial Software for Financial Advisors. Truth ConceptsTM. (n.d.). Retrieved Spring 2024, from https://truthconcepts.com/